To/

Happy 40th Birthday, take a look back in time to the year you were born 1983.

Love,

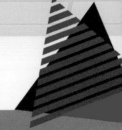

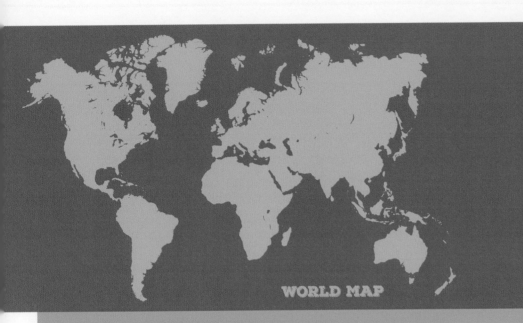

WORLD MAP

MAJOR WORLD LEADERS

UK- PRIME MINISTER - MARGARET THATCHER

US PRESIDENT - RONALD REAGAN

RUSSIA/SOVIET UNION - LEONID BREZHNEV, CHAIRMAN OF THE PEOPLE'S COMMISARS

SOUTH AFRICA - PRIME MINISTER - PIETER WILLEM BOTHA

ITALY - PRIME MINISTER - GIOVANNI SPADOLINI

GERMANY - CHANCELLOR - HELMUT SCHMIDT

FROM 1ST OCT HELMUT KOHL

FRANCE - PRIME MINISTER - FRANCOIS MITTERAND

CANADA - PRIME MINISTER - PIERRE TRUDEAU

CHINA - HEAD OF STATE - CHAIRMAN OF THE PEOPLE'S REPUBLIC OF CHINA POST ABOLISHED

PRESIDENT OF MEXICO   PRESIDENT - JOSE LOPEZ PORTILLO

JAPAN - PM - ZENKO SUZUKI

AUSTRALIA - PRIME MINISTER MALCOLM FRAZER

World Population

4.5 BILLION

Britain population

56.3 MILLION

2022

World Population

7.8 BILLION

Britain population

67.61

YOU HAVE BEEN LOVED FOR

40 years

THATS 480 MONTHS

2087 WEEKS

14,609 days

350,632 hrs

21,037,968

MINUTES

1,261,440,000

seconds

AND COUNTING...

BORN IN 1983

TOP TEN 80s OSCARS WINNERS

Out Of Africa (1985) - The movie grossed $227 million worldwide and earned an seven awards at the 58th Academy Awards.

Driving Miss Daisy (1989) Grossing $145 million securing 4 wins at the 62nd Academy Awards - Best Makeup, Screenplay Based on Material from Another Medium, Actress for Jessica Tandy, and Best Picture.

Terms Of Endearment (1983) 56th Academy Awards, earning an impressive eleven nominations and five wins. These included Best Screenplay Based on Material from Another Medium, Supporting Actor for Jack Nicholson, Actress for Shirley MacLaine, Director for Brooks, and Best Picture.

The Last Emperor (1987) it is the most awarded film of the 1980s, taking home nine Oscars at the 60th Academy Awards. These included Best Sound, Original Score, Film Editing, Costume Design, Cinematography, Art Direction, Screenplay Based on Material from Another Medium, Director for Bernardo Bertolucci, and Best Picture.

E.T. The Extra-Terrestrial (1982)
Won four - Best Visual Effects, Sound, Sound Effects Editing, and Original Score.

Gandhi (1982) Gandhi earned eight wins . These included; Film Editing, Cinematography, Art Direction, Costume Design, Screenplay, Actor for Ben Kingsley, Director for Attenborough, and Best Picture.

Rain Man (1988) Hotly anticipated movie of the 61st Academy Awards, earning eight nominations and four wins - the most of any movie that night.

Platoon (1986) Grossing an low to average $138million It enjoyed more success at the Oscars where it earned four wins.

Amadeus (1984) the big hit of '84.
- the second most of the 1980s. These included Best Costume Design, Makeup, Sound, Art Direction, Screenplay Based on Material from Another Medium, Actor for F. Murray Abraham, Director for Miloš Forman, and Best Picture.

Raiders Of The Lost Ark (1981)
Enjoyed a successful 54th Academy Awards, winning five. These included Best Art, Direction, Sound, Film Editing, and Visual Effects, and it was also the recipient of a Special Achievement Academy Award for Sound Effects Editing.

- Star Wars: Episode VI - Return of the Jedi
- Tootsie
- Flashdance
- Trading Places
- Wargames
- Octopussy
- Staying Alive
- Risky Business
- Mr.Mom
- National Lampoons vacation

80s

Breakfast Club

Director & writer: John Hughes

Stars: Emilio Estevez, Judd Nelson, Molly Ringwald

Beverley Hills Cop

Director: Martin Brest

Writers: Daniel Petrie Jr. (screenplay by), Danilo Bach

Stars: Eddie Murphy, Judge Reinhold, John Ashton

ET

Director: Steven Spielberg, Writer: Melissa Mathison

Stars: Henry Thomas, Drew Barrymore, Peter Coyote

Star Wars - the Empire strikes back

Director: Irvin Kershner, Writer: Leigh Brackett

FILMS

Top Gun

Director: Tony Scott,

Writers: Jim Cash, Jack Epps Jr.

Stars: Tom Cruise, Tim Robbins, Kelly McGillis.

Back to the Future

Director: Robert Zemeckis, writers: Robert Zemeckis, Bob Gale

Stars: Michael J. Fox, Christopher Lloyd, Lea Thompson

Ghost Busters

Director: Ivan Reitman, writers: Dan Aykroyd, Harold Ramis

Stars: Bill Murray, Dan Aykroyd, Sigourney Weaver

Caddyshack

Director: Harold Ramis, writers: Brian Doyle-Murray, Harold Ramis

Stars: Chevy Chase, Rodney Dangerfield, Bill Murray

Die Hard

Director: John McTiernan, writers: Roderick Thorp

Stars: Bruce Willis, Alan Rickman, Bonnie Bedelia

Ferris Buellers Day Off (1986)

Director & Writer: John Hughes, Stars: Matthew Broderick, Alan Ruck, Mia Sara

Britain's conservative government removed the Eady Levy. This was a subsidy for British film production. New projects were negatively affected by this. Box office income was also affected by the increasing quality and availability of TV programs. The American film industry was moving toward studio-driven films. There was a shift away from the filmmaker-driven films of the 1970s. Blockbuster hits were the only way to combat falling incomes. Studio marketing departments were encouraged to package neatly "high concept" films. The goal was to convey the essence of the movie in a single line and ensure full houses. A general broadening of acceptable standards was another change in the industry.

The formality of filmmaking is lessened with some boundaries being challenged. As the decade progressed, nudity in films increased. There was an increase in expectations and reliance on franchise films. Horror, science fiction, and action genres were particularly affected. Film producers embraced the Star Wars franchise format with open arms. The PG13 rating was introduced in 1984. This was done to address the difficulties in films between PG and R. Some of these difficulties were caused by films like Indiana Jones and the Temple of Doom and Gremlins (both 1984).

Star Wars: Episode VI – Return of the Jedi

The biggest film of 1983 It had a whopping budget of $32,500,000.

Grossing $309million it was a box office hit.

Movie Trivia

Mechanised mechanisms allowed the Emperor's chair to rotate as needed. Ian McDiarmid had to shuffle his feet to make the mechanism move since it never worked properly. To prevent the camera from seeing it, he used tape on the floor to tell him when to stop.

50 TOP GROSSING FILMS

Do you know how many of the decade's top-grossing films you have seen? Take a look at the list below to find out. Almost every 80s kid will have ticked off at least half of these items. Have you ticked off more than 40? Your knowledge of 80s movies is impressive.

1. Indiana Jones and the Last Crusade   Paramount $474,171,806   1989
2. Batman   Warner Bros. $411,348,924   1989
3. E.T. the Extra-Terrestrial   Universal Pictures $359,197,037   1982
4. Rain Man   MGM $354,825,435   1988
5. Back to the Future Part II   Universal $331,950,002   1989
6. Who Framed Roger Rabbit   Buena Vista/Touchstone Pictures $329,803,958   1988
7. Look Who's Talking   TriStar $296,999,813   1989
8. Coming to America   Paramount $288,752,301   1988
9. Return of the Jedi   20th Century Fox $252,583,617   1983
10. Crocodile Dundee II   Paramount $239,606,210   1988
11. Dead Poets Society   Buena Vista/Touchstone Pictures $235,860,116   1989
12. Beverly Hills Cop   Paramount Pictures $234,760,478   1984
13. Ghostbusters   Columbia Pictures $229,242,989   1984
14. Lethal Weapon 2   Warner Bros. $227,853,986   1989
15. Honey, I Shrunk the Kids   Buena Vista/Disney $222,724,172   1989
16. Twins   Universal $216,614,388   1988
17. Ghostbusters II   Columbia $215,394,738   1989
18. Raiders of the Lost Ark   Paramount Pictures $212,222,025   1981
19. Back to the Future   Universal Pictures $210,609,762   1985
20. The Empire Strikes Back   20th Century Fox $209,398,025   1980
21. Rambo III   Carolco $189,015,611   1988
22. The Little Mermaid   Buena Vista/Disney $184,155,863   1989
23. Indiana Jones and the Temple of Doom   Paramount Pictures $179,870,271   1984
24. A Fish Called Wanda   MGM $177,889,000   1988
25. Tootsie   Columbia Pictures $177,200,000   1982
26. Top Gun   Paramount Pictures $176,781,728   1986
27. Crocodile Dundee   Paramount Pictures $174,803,506   1986
28. Cocktail   Buena Vista/Touchstone Pictures $171,504,781   1988
29. Three Men and a Baby   Buena Vista/Touchstone Pictures $167,780,960   1987
30. Fatal Attraction   Paramount Pictures $156,645,693   1987
31. Beverly Hills Cop II   Paramount Pictures $153,665,036   1987
32. Gremlins   Warner Bros. $153,083,102   1984
33. Born on the Fourth of July   Universal $161,001,698   1989
34. Big   20th Century Fox $151,668,774   1988
35. Rambo: First Blood Part II   Carolco Pictures $150,415,432   1985
36. Die Hard   20th Century Fox $140,767,956   1988
37. The Naked Gun: From the Files of Police Squad!   Paramount $140,000,000   1988
38. Platoon   Orion Pictures $138,530,565   1986
39. An Officer and a Gentleman   Paramount Pictures $129,795,554   1982
40. Rocky IV   Metro-Goldwyn-Mayer $127,873,716   1985
41. Rocky III   Metro-Goldwyn-Mayer $124,146,897   1982
42. Good Morning, Vietnam   Buena Vista/Touchstone Pictures $123,922,370   1987
43. On Golden Pond   Universal Pictures $119,285,432   1981
44. The Karate Kid Part II   Columbia Pictures $115,103,979   1986
45. Star Trek IV: The Voyage Home   Paramount Pictures $109,713,132   1986
46. Terms of Endearment   Paramount Pictures $108,423,489   1983
47. Superman II   Warner Bros. $108,185,706   1981
48. Porky's   20th Century Fox $105,492,483   1982
49. 9 to 5   20th Century Fox $103,290,500   1980
50. Stir Crazy   Columbia Pictures $101,300,000   1980

AVERAGE COST OF LIVING 1983

Average House £23,944
in todays money thats approx £102,500
Average Salary £7,617
in today's money thats approx £31,300
Average Car Price £4,550
[Ford Sierra £6,924]
in today's money thats approx £18,000
Weekly Family Food bill £36
in today's money thats £142

Item	1983 Price	Today's Money
Can of coke	£0.20	£0.87 in today's money
Loaf of Bread	£0.39	£1.69 in today's money
A dozen eggs	£0.73	£3.16 in today's money
2lb sugar	£0.44	£1.91 in today's money
1pt Milk	£0.30	£1.30 in today's money
Lb bananas	£0.32	£1.39 in today's money
Mars bar	£0.16	£0.69 in today's money
100g maxwell coffee	£0.84	£3.64 in today's money
Pint of beer	£0.50	£2.17 in today's money
Digestive biscuits	£0.20	£0.87 in today's money
Odeon cinema ticket	£1.65	£7.15 in today's money
Levi jeans	£20	£86.63 in today's money

Spaceflight of the first woman from the United States

As the third woman in history to go to space, Sally Ride made history in 1983. On STS-7, the physicist crewed the space shuttle Challenger. She assisted in the launch of two satellites and operated the shuttle's robotic arm. When asked about the experience, she said, "The thing I'll remember most about the flight is that it was fun. In fact, I'm sure it was the most fun I'll ever have in my life."

Madonna released her self-titled album in the Summer of 1983 and "Holiday" became her first Hot 100 single. A career that has spanned decades, providing us with some of the most memorable music videos, fresh looks, and a variety of music styles.

Did you know? You know!

During the Motown 25 TV special, Michael Jackson performed the moonwalk for the first time. As a result, it became a must-learn dance move for kids and young adults, and a signature move at his concerts.

Mario Bros

As part of Nintendo's arcade game line, Mario Bros was released in 1983. Nintendo's chief engineer, Gunpei Yokoi, and Shigeru Miyamoto designed it. Mario and Luigi are Italian twin brothers who exterminate sewer creatures by knocking them upside-down and kicking them. This is Intelligent Systems' first game for the Famicom/Nintendo Entertainment System. A spin-off from the Donkey Kong series, it became part of the Mario franchise.

MUSIC

EURYTHMICS

THEHUMANLEAGUE

ULTRAVOX

NEVERGONNAGIVE
YOUUPNEVERGONN
ALETYOUDOWNNEV
ERGONNARUNARO
UNDANDDESERTYO
UNEVERGONNAMA
KEYOUCRYNEVERG
ONNASAYGOODBYE
NEVERGONNATELL
ALIEANDHURTYOU

SPANDAUBALLET

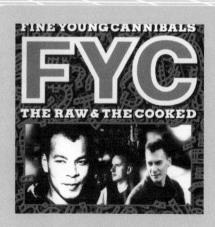

'80S MUSIC
Diverse, Eclectic & Extravagant

In the 1980s, British acts took the American market by storm with the 2nd wave of the British Invasion. The development and promotion of these upcoming bands was heavily influenced by MTV. It was mostly synthpop and new wave artists that benefited from this increased exposure. Madonna, Prince, Michael Jackson, Culture Club, and Wham benefitted from the popularity of MTV music videos. British music became increasingly popular abroad, leading to Indie Rock's rise. The dominance of record labels was shifting to local music scenes - Manchester in particular - and independent labels. An impressive yet not exhaustive list of 80s successful bands includes New Order, The Stone Roses, The Jesus and Mary Chain, The Cure, Guns & Roses, INXS, Pet Shop Boys, Public Enemy, and The Jam. There were several sounds associated with the 80s, including New Wave and the New Romantics. Glam rock fashions, frilly top shirts, and lots of eyeliner filled London's nightclubs. With a synthesiser, the New Romantics created a sound that has become synonymous with the era. Ultravox and Visage were among the pioneers of this new music. Top-charting bands included Adam and the Ants, Culture Club, Spandeau Ballet, and Duran Duran. The 80s saw the continuation of some of the most successful punk bands. The Psychedelic Furs and Siouxsie and the Banshees continued to enjoy success well into the 1980s.

09.01.83	Phil Collins	You can't hurry love
23.01.83	Men at Work	Down Under
13.02.83	Kajagoogoo	Too Shy
27.02.83	Michael Jackson	Billie Jean
06.03.83	Bonnie Tyler	Total Eclipse of the Heart
20.03.83	Duran Duran	Is there something I should know
13.04.83	Bucks Fizz	The Camera Never Lies
03.04.83	David Bowie	Let's Dance
24.04.83	Spandeau Ballet	True
22.05.83	New Edition	Candy Girl
29.05.83	The Police	Every Breath you Take
26.06.83	Rod Stewart	Baby Jane
17.07.83	Paul Young	Wherever I Lay my Hat
07.08.83	KC and the Sunshine Band	Give it Up
28.08.83	UB40	Red Red Wine
18.09.83	Culture Club	Karma Chameleon
30.10.83	Billy Joes	Uptown Girl
04.12.83	The Flying Pickets	Only You

The 1980s conjure up images of lycra, neon colours, shoulder pads, massive hair, leg warmers, shell suits, and many other bizarre fashions. Bold style, vibrant colours, and larger-than-life silhouettes characterized the 1980s. Whether it was power dressing, aerobic leisure wear, or new romanticism, it was all very over the top.

Which of these trends can you spot in your childhood family photos?

Despite being too young to sport a perm, you may remember your mum's perm and longing for one.

Oh, the good old scrunchie. A colourful hair accessory that can also be used as a decorative fabric bracelet. Classy!

The slogan T-shirt remained a fashion staple for the majority of the decade and is still popular today. There were many, many versions of thought-provoking or funny slogans, but Frankie Says Relax is probably the most famous. Originally symbolizing psychedelic drug culture, smiley faces moved into mainstream culture in the 1970s and became the base of our love of emojis today!

It is impossible to talk about the 1980s without mentioning spandex or Lycra. What about those of you who owned full spandex outfits?! At the time, it must have looked gorgeous. In the 1980s, velour was popularized by designer brands like Christian Dior and supported by high-street brands. In the 1980s, Vivienne Westwood was a key figure in the "New Romanticism" fashion movement, whose designs became household names. She is widely credited with bringing punk and new-wave fashion to the mainstream.

Anything with animal prints - jackets, coats, socks, hats, etc. Animal prints were seen in fashion before the 1980s, but they were one of the most enduring trends of the decade. Earrings of the 80s were big and bold - gold hoops, long dangling sparkles. Just like the hairstyles!

I ♥ the 80's

FASHION

NOW

THAT'S WILD FASHION

80s

- Power suits
- Shell suits
- Knitted jumpers
- Bright prints
- 2 piece casual-wear
- Washed-out denim

TRANSPORT

UK's top 10 best-selling cars of the 1980s to give you a snapshot of the decade.

1) Ford Escort. Ford launched the Escort in 1968 as a replacement for the ancient Anglia.

3) Ford Fiesta.

4) Austin/MG Metro.

5) Ford Sierra.

6) Vauxhall Astra.

7) Ford Cortina.

8) Ford Orion.

10) Vauxhall Nova.

SPORTS

Association football

- UEFA championships league - Hamburg 1-0   Juventus

- FA Cup - Manchester United won

- Cup Winners' Cup – Aberdeen 2-1 Real Madrid

- Scotland – Dundee United won the First Division

Cycling

Giro d'Italia won by Giuseppe Saronni of Italy

Tour de France – aurent Fignon of France

Golf

Men's professional

- Masters Tournament – Seve Ballesteros

- U.S. Open – Larry Nelson

- British Open – Tom Watson

- PGA Championship – Hal Sutton

- PGA Tour money leader – Hal Sutton ($426,668)

- Senior PGA Tour money leader – Don January ($237,571)

Men's amateur

- British Amateur - Philip Parkin

- U.S. Amateur - Jay Sigel

Women's professional

- LPGA Championship – Patty Sheehan

- U.S. Women's Open – Jan Stephenson

- Classique Peter Jackson Classic – Hollis Stacy

- LPGA Tour money leader – JoAnne Carner ($291,404)

Horse racing

- Cheltenham Gold Cup – Bregawn

- Grand National –Corbiere

Flat races

- Australia – Melbourne Cup won by Kiwi

- Canada – Queen's Plate won by Bompago

- France – Prix de l'Arc de Triomphe won by All Along

- Ireland – Irish Derby Stakes - Shareef Dancer

- Japan – Japan Cup - Stanerra

Grand Slam in tennis men's results:

- Australian Open – Mats Wilander

- French Open – Yannick Noah

- Wimbledon championships – John McEnroe

- US Open – Jimmy Connors

Grand Slam in tennis women's results:

- Australian Open – Martina Navratilova

- French Open – Chris Evert

- Wimbledon championships – Martina Navratilova

- US Open – Martina Navratilova

TV news 1980s

Colour TV was introduced in the UK in 1967 and became increasingly popular throughout the 1970s. Colour sets did not overtake black & white sets until 1976. By the early 1980s, almost no one used black and white TVs.

Unique things of '80s TV

There were numerous instances of TV breakdowns - programmes were often just lost completely and replaced with some light melody.

Before closing down at midnight, the BBC would play the national anthem.

Ceefax and Teletext - book holidays, check the weather and play games. This is the 80s version of the internet. In 2012, this service came to an end.

Testcard - remember the little girl with the chalkboard when no programmes were on?

Public information advertisements are horrendous. During the day, people are shown electrocutions, mothers under train carriages, and all of these things to terrify them into compliance.

Notable events from the decade.

The wedding of Prince Charles and Princess Diana in 1981 was watched by 750 million people.

Breakfast TV debuts in 1983.

Sky TV begins broadcasting in 1989.

Popular 80s TV Shows

1980s Viewing Chart Toppers:

Dallas [BBC1, November 22 1980]: 21.60 million
Coronation Street [ITV, January 16 1985]: 20.60 million
Bread [BBC1, December 11 1988]: 20.95 million

From 1989 to 1996, Challenge Anneka aired on television. In her role as 'Skyrunner', Anneka Rice provided years of excitement for young television viewers.

Channel 4 broadcast Minipops in 1983. Kids singing pop hits to brightly colored sets and music aimed at younger viewers proved to be a successful formula for this kids television show.

A thrilling race against the clock awaits you in The Interceptor. It's chaotic but addictive to watch contestants run through fields while carrying huge backpacks!

Channel 4 launched Countdown in 1982. The show was co-presented by Carol Vordermann for 26 years. It still stands strong today.

The most ridiculous prizes of any game show, presented by Terry Wogan from 1977-1983, make Blankety Blank comedy gold.

From 1981 to 1991, Bergerac was a sports-car-driving detective on BBC television 'dramatic drama'.

Cilla Black presented Blind Date with the question, "What's your name and where are you from?" Over the course of the program's run, it aired from 1985 to 2003.

Only Fools and Horses – aired in 1981, still comedy gold today.
Cheers was a bar where everyone knew your name. A family favorite for Friday night viewing. Starring Nicholas Colasanto, Ted Danson, Shelley Long, John Ratzenberger & Rhea Perlman.

Fame's line "Fame costs – and here's where it begins paying" will be familiar to anyone who has watched the show.

hael Thomas and Don Johnson rolled up their sleeves in 1984 Miami Vice

Channel 4 broadcast Desmond's from 1989 to 1994.

New breakfast shows were aired by the BBC and ITV in 1983. Michael Parkinson, David Frost, Angela Rippon, Anna Ford, and Robert Kee are the ITV presenters team.

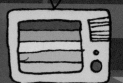

Are you ready for a major dose of nostalgia? Cartoons from the 1980s shaped an entire generation. You could dream of hanging out with the chipmunk brothers, drinking Gummiberry juice, or becoming a stealthy turtle who enjoyed eating pizza in gutters in the 80s. Danger Mouse 1981-1991. They were a hilarious crime-fighting duo, Danger Mouse and Penfold. Count Duckula, one of the villains, got his own show because he was so popular. The Smurfs 1981-1989. A huge success for the tiny blue people who lived in mushroom-shaped houses in the forest.

1983-1985: He-Man and the Masters of the Universe. Bythe power of Greyskull! This was one of the first animated shows produced solely to sell toys.

Super Ted 1982-1986. Taking a broken teddy bear to a magic cloud where Mother Nature gives him special powers, a spotty alien's cosmic dust brings him back to life. It's a wonderfully weird cartoon that's become a cult classic. Did you have SuperTed vitamins? 1984-1986: Trap Door. Do you remember the theme tune to this cartoon? ... The claymation series featured comedy and scare tactics as strange creatures escaped from the Trap Door and caused chaos for Berk, the blobby blue assistant to the Lovecraftian "thing upstairs".

From 1983 to 1986, Inspector Gadget was on television. In this hilarious cartoon, Detective Gadget is oblivious to the dangers around him. Did you covet Penny's computer book?

The Transformers, 1984-1987. Extraterrestrial robots that can transform into cars, trucks, and other vehicles - pretty much anything really! From 1985 to 1988, Jem and the Holograms aired. A rock star with a secret identity. There was nobody who didn't want to be Jem.

Do you remember?

The Gummi Bears were on the air from 1985 to 1991. It was Disney's first attempt at an animated series of full length. It was a favourite among 80s kids.

From 1983 to 1986, Bananaman was on the air. Eric Wimp becomes Bananaman when he eats a banana. He is a powerful superhero with unique gadgets (remember the banana laser gun and banana thermal gun?).

Count Duckula 1988-1993. This power-hungry villain was never quite able to achieve his world dominance goals.

Care Bears 1984-1988. The Care Bears taught kids the importance of friendship and kindness. Through the 80s, care bear teddy bears were a top sellers on Christmas lists because of their cuteness and cuddliness.

SheRa Princess of Power 1985. The Spin-off of He-Man was aimed at girls as a counterbalance to the boy-centric series.

A Pup Named Scooby-Doo 1988-1991. The 60s and 70s classic Scooby-Doo was brought to a whole new generation through A Pup Named Scooby-Doo.

Chip & Dales Rescue Rangers 1989-1990. Attempting to replicate DuckTales' success, Disney created Chip & Dale, a series based on two of its favourite characters.

The Snorks 1984-1989. Snorks are an underwater version of The Smurfs. Over the 5 years it broadcast, it wasn't quite as popular, but it was still enjoyed.

Thundercats 1985-1990. A group of cat-like aliens escape to Third Earth as their home world is destroyed. One of our favourite theme tunes...Thunder, Thunder, Thunder, Thunder Cats! Don't be shy, sing along...

Teenage Mutant Ninja Turtles 1987-1996.

'80s Childhood

How did you spend your time before the internet?

If you have children or know someone who has children, you may have been asked this question. To kids now, it seems impossible that there were only four channels on TV. You had to rush home to watch your favourite cartoon at the time it was broadcast. No iPads? What a horror!

With a confident attitude, the 1980s began. We thought we could accomplish anything because of the successful space race of the 1960s and the technological advancements of the 1970s. In the 1980s, many areas of life were characterised by this spirit of exuberance.

The decade was characterized by consumption and materialism.

When kids were growing up in the 1980s, they played on the streets without having 'playdates' with their friends. A generation of people who grew up in the 1980s is the last to have grown up without being strongly influenced by the internet. Children of this generation are the last to experience a childhood free from modern technology, as well as teenage years untethered from social media.

Kids of the 1980s had Barbies & Ken, were enthralled by Teenage Mutant Ninja Turtles, had cabbage patch dolls, and practically everyone wished for a Nintendo. As technology developed, toys became increasingly electrical. Their size, brightness, and boldness increased. Musical instruments and talking dolls were popular with children. Rubix cubes were and still are a national favourite.

It is impossible to describe childhood without mentioning sweets. Some of the retro confections included refresher chewy sweets, space hoppers, double dips, and everlasting gobstoppers. Your neighbourhood ice-cream van may have sold these if you were lucky. In a small paper bag, 10 penny sweets are randomly selected for a 10 penny mix up, the most popular van sweet. These days, it's rare to see an ice-cream van that isn't stationary in a park or leisure facility. We've lost some things - Coconut Boost, Old Jamaica & Twilight bars.

It might surprise you to learn that the half penny was still in circulation in 1982! 1984 marked the end of its service. Children kept in touch for years on end through international penpal programs set up by schools during the decade. Pong, the mind-blowing arcade game from Atari, made it possible to play arcade-style games at home. Then came Donkey Kong and Super Mario Brothers from Nintendo. The gaming industry was born under your watch.

We were told as children that we would be taking holidays on the moon by the turn of the century, have flying cars, and fashion would be extraterrestrial. Despite not reaching that goal, I'm sure you never imagined the technology you would have access to and how it would change the world.

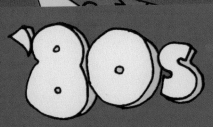 80s toys

The iconic toy of the 1980s, the Bluebird Big Yellow Teapot was released by Bluebird in 1981.

• Masters of the Universe: The Power of He-Man. During the decade, He-Man was one of the most successful franchises. The decade saw the release of many toy figures, action games, and playsets.

Fisher Price produced many of the most memorable toys of the 1980s. The most popular toys can be found below. Are there any of these in your old family pictures?

- Fisher Price extendable skates
- Fisher Price Music Box Record Player
- Fisher Price Classic Chatter phone
- Fisher Price aeroplane
- Fisher Price service station
- Fisher Price cassette player

• Ghostbusters toys - following the release of the 1984 film, Ghostbusters toys topped many Christmas lists.

Transformers join the ranks of memorable childhood toys. Ever since they were first released in the 1980s, they have remained a top choice on childhood wishlists.

- Kellogs bike reflector (1988-1990)
- TOMY Lights Alive
- Elmo has been a favourite since Sesame Street first aired in the 1960s. The most coveted character was Elmo.

The Gremlins were released in 1984. In the years following the film's success, Gremlin plush toys flew off the shelves.

Christmas List Favourites 1983

- Stompers Truck £1.99 (approx £10 today).
- G.I Joe Figures £1.20 (approx. £5 today).
- BMX bike £45 (approx. £220 today).
- Glo Worm £4.99 (approx £20 today).
- Commodore 64 £117 (approx. £500 today).
- Care Bear £17 (approx £55 today)
- Cabbage Patch Doll £15 (approx. £50 today).
- My Little Pony £4 (approx £20 today).
- Rainbow Brite £12.99 (approx £45 today).

Hasbro Playskool's Glo Worm. 1982 release. A bedtime favourite.

• Texas Instruments' Speak & Spell. It was a handheld electronic computer that was released in the late 1970s.

NES - Nintendo Entertainment System - released 1985 in America, distributed in Europe in Back in the day, the NES cost around £80, approximately £320 in today's currency.

in 1986/87. which is

'80s Toys

Do you remember?

1983 WORLD EVENTS

U.S Embassy is bombed in Beirut

A Terrorist attack by a suicide bomber on the U.S Embassy in Beirut, killing 63 people.

Richard Noble land speed record

As he drove Thrust 2 in the Black Rock Desert, Nevada, Richard Noble set a new land speed record of 633.468 mph.

Unemployment Rises in the US to 12 million the highest figure since 1941.

The Worlds Population is estimated at 4.72 billion

China's Population reaches 1 billion

HBO premieres Fraggle Rock in January 1983.

Henson created and produced the show, one of HBO's first original programs.

- A group of muppets called Fraggles interacted with other groups within their world in Fraggle Rock.
- While all the groups depended on each other for survival, many of the episodes featured conflicts between the Fraggles and the other groups.
- There were 96 episodes of Fraggle Rock and it aired until 1987.
- The show was broadcast in nearly one hundred countries around the world, as its creators hoped to promote world peace.

Cruise Missiles

The US deploys **Cruise Missiles** in Europe at the Greenham Common Air Force Base in England and Deploys **Pershing Missiles** in West Germany Due to the deployment of Cruise Missiles in the UK CND organises marches and rallies with over 200,000 attending.

Rhodesia / Zimbabwe
Civil War breaks out in Zimbabwe

UK Seatbelt Law
Seatbelt use for drivers and front seat passengers becomes mandatory in the United Kingdom.

Earthquake New York
A 5.2 earthquake hits Central New York

Mario Bros.
Game Debuts
In Japan, Mario Bros. was released as an arcade game during July. In addition to creating the Legend of Zelda and Donkey Kong, Shigeru Miyamoto also created Metroid and the Game Boy. Two plumbers, Mario and his brother Luigi, fought sewer creatures in New York in the Mario Bros. game. As the video game industry was going through a crash at the time of its release, the game was not initially successful, but Super Mario Bros. for the Nintendo Entertainment System (NES) console in 1985 made it a successful series of games.

Brinks Mat robbery - Brinks Mat warehouse robbery at Heathrow Airport making off with three tons of gold bars valued at $37.5 million

Maze High Security Prison - Mass prisoner breakout from Maze High Security Prison near Lisburn, Northern Ireland.

SDI, or Strategic Defense Initiative
The Strategic Defense Initiative (SDI) is proposed by Ronald Reagan.
A televised address by Ronald Reagan in March 1983 proposed the Strategic Defense Initiative (SDI).
Designed to intercept and prevent a nuclear missile attack by the Soviet Union on the U.S., the proposed defence system was a highly advanced system relying on technology not yet developed.
Some critics referred to the plan as "Star Wars" during this decade because they believed it would be impossible to implement with the current capabilities of technology.

There are now five classes of British nationality under the British Nationality Act 1981, which came into effect on January 1st 1983.

BBC broadcasts Breakfast Time for the first time on 17th Jan.

Seatbelts become mandatory on the 31st Jan, 11 years after they became mandatory equipment.

On 3rd February, unemployment reached a record high of 3,224,715

26th Feb - In English football, Pat Jennings, 37, becomes the first player to appear in 1,000 senior games.

In the United Kingdom, the compact disc (CD) goes on sale on 1st March.

26th March: Liverpool defeat Manchester United 2–1 in the final at Wembley Stadium to win the Football League Cup for the third time.

1st April: In protest at the placement of American nuclear weapons in British military bases, thousands form a 14-mile human chain.

21st April: England and Wales introduced the one-pound coin.

May -A general election is called for 9 June by Margaret Thatcher. In most polls, she is expected to win, with the Tories 8 to 12 points ahead of Labour

The Premier League championship is won by Liverpool on May 14th. Manager Bob Paisley steps down.

London uses wheel clamps for the first time to combat illegal parking on May 16th.

UK EVENTS 1983

With a majority of 144 seats, Margaret Thatcher, Conservative Prime Minister since 1979, wins a landslide victory in the general election.

BBC One broadcasts the first episode of historical sitcom Blackadder on June 15th.

A heatwave grips the country as temperatures in London reach 33°C on July 15th.

Aug 1st: Recession-induced slump in car sales leads to the launch of A-prefix car registration plates, helping the industry recover.

Social Services Secretary Norman Fowler predicts that privatising cleaning, catering, and laundering services will save between £90 and £180 million a year for the National Health Service.

Sep 22nd: Docklands redevelopment in East London begins with the opening of an Enterprise Zone on the Isle of Dogs.

Following Michael Foot's retirement, Neil Kinnock was elected leader of the Labour Party. The election was won by Kinnock by more than 70%.

22nd Oct: London's Campaign for Nuclear Disarmament march attracts over a million people against nuclear weapons.

In London, 6,800 gold bars worth nearly £26 million were stolen from the Brink's-Mat vault at Heathrow Airport in a Brink's-Mat robbery on November 26. Only two men are ever convicted of the crime, and only a fraction of the gold is ever recovered.

Dec 6th: Harefield Hospital performs Britain's first heart and lung transplant.

Dec 8th: Lords vote to allow TV broadcasts of their proceedings.

Dec 10th: Nobel Prize for Literature awarded to William Golding

'80S INVENTIONS

1982

Sony released the world's first compact disc player (the CDP-101). Originally marketed to the more affluent members of society, this product retailed for over £500. As with any other technology as time passed the technology became more affordable and moved to the mainstream.

The origins of disposable cameras can be traced back to the 1880s. The first commercial disposable camera was released by Kodak in 1987. When it was released in the US, it cost $6.95 and inspired a host of similar products by competitors. Market growth occurred between 1988 and 1992

In 1987, Prozac was introduced to the market after being tested by the FDA. Patients with depression began receiving the new medication from their doctors.

Jarvik 7

The world's first artificial heart was invented by Dr. Robert Jarvik. 2nd December 1982 marked the date when Dr. William De Vries successfully tested the device. The patient, Barney Clark, volunteered for the procedure. In the aftermath of its success, it became widely used as a temporary measure to keep patients alive while they waited for a real heart donor.

1989 – High-definition television was invented.

1983 – Soft bifocal contact lens was invented.

1987 – Disposable contact lenses were invented.

1982

Betamax cameras were originally released by Sony for news agencies. Soon, however, they began to see the potential for everyday consumer use. Within a year, they had refined the technology and promoted its release to consumers. Betamax and VHS competed fiercely. Betamax remained dominant for some time, but Panasonic released the VHS camcorder in 1985. Betamax's end was marked by this game changer.

'80S INVENTIONS

1985

Since 1985, Microsoft has released 10 major versions of Windows. A landmark moment in the history of the tech industry was the release of the first Windows operating system (led by Bill Gates). A mouse was incorporated into Windows 1 to allow users to input information. Information was primarily entered using keyboards until then.

1989

Nintendo released the Gameboy in 1985, allowing users to play a variety of games by swapping out cartridges.

1988

The invention of digital cellular phones.

12th August

A 16-bit operating system called MS-DOS 1.0 was introduced with the IBM "Personal Computer" in 1981, IBM's revolution in a box.

Apple Macintosh 1984

In 1984, Apple revolutionised the technology industry with the release of the MacIntosh, one of the world's first commercially successful personal computers. Unlike other Apple products at the time, the MacIntosh was finally a computer that the average person could utilise. In fact, Steve Jobs said the computer was to be used by the "person on the street."

Genetic engineering was used to create human growth hormone.

1986 Synthetic skin was invented by G. Gregory Gallico, III.

1984
LaserJet is a new printer from HP.

DNA Fingerprinting 1983

When Alec Jeffreys was studying hereditary family diseases (1984), he noticed a repetitive DNA pattern in humans. During further research at the University of Leicester, it was found that variations in DNA could be used to identify individuals (unless the individual had a twin). When two murders occurred near the university, he had the opportunity to test his claim. Genetic fingerprinting was the name he gave this new discovery.

Advertising in the 80s

The popularity of branded food products and brand loyalty were at their peak. The majority of households purchase branded food consumables. A striking difference from today's supermarket own-brand, lower-priced alternatives. A growing health consciousness was used by brands in their marketing; cluster bars were marketed as alternatives to chocolate, Horlicks' ad featured a woman doing aerobics, suggesting that it was a healthy option, Robinsons Bali water was marketed as a healthy food option with lots of fruit and no artificial ingredients, and Heinz's potato salad was presented as a healthy food choice. Advertisements in the 80s were still highly product-focused, but they also included more lifestyle marketing than in previous decades.

• SR toothpaste - no longer with us but was an '80s favourite.

• Primula cheese - a newly-released product on the market and a popular choice for buffets.

• Rayleigh bikes - do you remember these?

• Plumrose Ham - an outdated advertising approach.

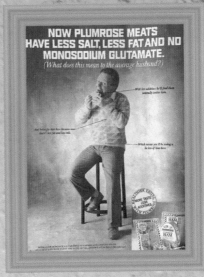

The legal stuff

Attribution for photo images goes to the following talented photographers under the creative commons licenses specified:

Printed in Great Britain
by Amazon

34298878R00025